Arthur Edward John Legge

Sunshine and Smoke

A Book of Verse

Arthur Edward John Legge

Sunshine and Smoke
A Book of Verse

ISBN/EAN: 9783337339302

Printed in Europe, USA, Canada, Australia, Japan

Cover: Foto ©Thomas Meinert / pixelio.de

More available books at **www.hansebooks.com**

SUNSHINE AND SMOKE

A Book of Verse

By

ARTHUR E. J. LEGGE

LONDON : SIMPKIN, MARSHALL & CO.
STATIONERS' HALL COURT, & SOLD
BY HATCHARDS, PICCADILLY . . 1895

CONTENTS

CHRISTMAS IN HYDE PARK

BEYOND the net-work of the thin black branches
  Hangs the white sun upon a pallid sky,
      And, like the ghostly smile we sometimes trace
      Fading half-formed upon a woman's face,
The bloodless glimmer of the beams it launches
      Seems to grow cold and die.

Smoke-stained, impenetrable walls of vapour
  Shorten our vision with fantastic frown,
      Hiding the formal paths and stiff expanse
      Of turf too neatly tended, save where chance
Has left a few dead leaves like scraps of paper,
      Crumpled and dry and brown.

Poor imitation is this landscape yonder
  Of that which ought to soothe our eyes to-day ;
      And yet some broken line, some varied tint,
      May stir our thoughts with a suggested hint,
Open a door, and let our fancies wander
      To visions far away.

A little make-believe will soon transfigure
  The fog's dark drapery to wreathes of mist
      In soft pure circles on a rounded hill,
      Where fern and sedge and tussock lie so still,
Helpless beneath the morning's frozen rigour,
      But by the sunbeams kissed.

The hoary rime appears to bend the bracken,
  Cresting with white its vague and neutral brown,
    And frosted flakes are powdered on the grass,—
    Tears dropped by winter-fairies as they pass,—
Whilst ivy tendrils on the oak-bark slacken,
  And mistletoe droops down.

Beneath the taper arms of smooth-skinned beeches
  The flush of fallen leaves is scarcely seen ;
    And, near at hand, the same white foam has hid
    Pale acorn-shell, and yellow chestnut-lid,
And moss that o'er the rotten tree stump reaches,
  Russet and gold and green.

No more we shudder at discordant riot
  Of jarring voice, quick foot, and restless wheel.
    The spell has made us deaf to every sound
    That groans and mutters in the streets around ;
And on our dreamland is a holy quiet,
  A calm that we can feel.

Nought speaks, save noisy rooks their passage winging
  With stately flight across the distant plough,
    Or blackbird in the leafless garden-hedge,
    Or wild-fowl hidden at the water's edge,
Or church-bells in the lonely village ringing,
  Behind the upland's brow.

Then through the park it seems that there come
      trooping
  Stout, broad-faced fellows, firm of chest and limb,—
    Each laden with a time-worn instrument,
    Cracked violin, or cornet bruised and bent,—
They halt, and, in the feeble sunshine grouping,
  They sing an old-world hymn.

Harsh and untrained the music of their voices ;
   Still harsher the companion chords they play ;
      And yet the notes of that familiar air
      Seem to have found an echo everywhere,
Till one might fancy Nature's self rejoices
      That Christ was born to-day.

Fresh pictures follow as our thoughts go rushing
   Down the broad track our memories unfold ; —
      Lightly we pass through rutted country lanes,
      By cottage walls, darkened with weather-stains,
And hedges where the holly-berries blushing
      Gleam in the sun's pale gold.

We reach the little unfrequented village,
   Crowned with its scanty stems of curling smoke,
      Where, here and there, against a garden-gate,
      Which creaks its apprehension of his weight,
One of the strong, ungainly sons of tillage
      Leans like a knotted oak.

One spirit is awakened at each meeting,
   One custom spreads its sceptre over all ;—
      The grave slow smile that stirs the solemn face,
      The dumb salute, given with clownish grace,
And then the well-remembered English greeting,
      Framed for the festival.

And, while its echoes in our hearts are ringing,
   We tread the churchyard path, between the graves
      That mutely mock life's pompous little hour,
      And reach the open door beneath the tower,
From which the bells a load of sound are flinging
      In molten, measured waves.

Softly we enter, for that homely place is
   Strange and unearthly in the dusky light
     That filters through the narrow panes, and falls
     On flagged white floor and tablet-covered walls,
And plays upon the simple, rugged faces
   Which meet our roving sight.

Their ears drink in the accents unaffected
   Of one whom Fate has surely sent to them
     As fitted such a backward flock to teach,—
     Unlearned, sympathetic, plain of speech,—
Within whose gentle eyes we see reflected
   The star of Bethlehem.

We drop the veil ; 'twere meaningless to linger
   Among the ghosts of matters dead and gone.
     The lost illusions fade into the mist,
     Time's sheeted form has clasped us by the wrist,
And, pointing forward with its spectral finger,
   Motions us always on.

New voices speak to us, new lamps are shining ;
   The curtain lifts upon an altered scene ;
     The play has entered on another act,
     And we were wiser to accept the fact,
With no vain tears, no profitless repining
   Over what must have been.

Perchance there may be here and there a relic
   Of customs which the ages have outworn ;
     In far-off valleys, on secluded hills,
     The heart within some blameless bosom thrills
To hear the harmony of songs angelic
   Hailing the Christmas morn.

Lingering freaks of morris-dance and mummer,
  Feudal festivities, unbounded cheer,
    Still mark the season in some distant place,
    That lags behind its fellows in the race,—
Just as the glories of St. Martin's summer
  Gild the declining year.

But life's half-liquid substance ever changes ;
  Fresh particles come surging to the top ;
    Old bonds are broken, old conditions die,
    Yesterday's truth becomes to-morrow's lie,
And, in the market of the world's exchanges,
  New values rise and drop.

There are no final answers to the questions ;
  No formula can make the problems plain ;
    After long centuries have beaten out
    Systems and creeds, the deathless voice of doubt
Breathes but a whisper of its vague suggestions,
  And scatters all again.

The lofty faith which led the march of nations
  Sinks from its post appointed in the van,
    And other flags are carried to the front,
    And other fighters bear the battle's brunt,
Casting new light upon the old relations
  Fixed between man and man.

Each altered movement in the game is greeted
  With the hot clamour that assailed the last ;—
    Some, flushed with victory, proclaim the birth
    Of Progress, Brotherhood, and Heaven on Earth,
Whilst others, listless, sullen, and defeated,
  Sadly bemoan the past.

Better to stand aloof from either faction,
　　Seeing how every sun that rises sets ;—
　　　　The pendulum with ordered motion swings,
　　　　And we poor puppets, when Fate pulls the strings,
May feel the play of action and reaction,
　　　　Unmoved by vain regrets.

Why should we deal the world another measure
　　Than that with which our hearts are satisfied ?
　　　　We do not fear to face the common truth,
　　　　Nor weep because the freshness of our youth,
Worn with experience of pain and pleasure,
　　　　Sadly has drooped and died.

We have not grudged inevitable payment
　　For scanty gifts the niggard Fates allow ;
　　　　We have not grieved that knowledge must be
　　　　　　bought
　　　　With branded scars of suffering and thought,
Nor murmured since our once unspotted raiment
　　　　Is soiled and tattered now.

We take the cup nor flinch because its sweetness
　　Is mingled with the bitterness of gall ;
　　　　If it should not be seasoned to our taste,
　　　　'Twere madness still to let it run to waste,
And we will drink the draught in its completeness,
　　　　Or touch it not at all.

Though faith be withered in the flame of reason,
　　Though love be sullied with the lees of lust,
　　　　Though all the hopes that seemed to promise fair
　　　　Should end in disappointment and despair,
Cowards alone would count it less than treason
　　　　To grovel in the dust.

Each smarting failure has in turn afforded
  Incentives to support us in the strife ;—
    The soldier, when the hard-fought conflict ends,
    Viewing the corpses that were once his friends,
  Could scarcely wish the triumph unrecorded
    To bring them back to life.

And though the dreamy shadow-land we grew in
  Smiles to us sadly through the faded years,
    And eyelids for one moment may be wet,
    It is not with the weakness of regret,
  But only as some ivy-covered ruin
    Often will move our tears.

No weakness !—ah, no weakness !—still unbroken
  We watch the cloaked assailants round us creep.
    The past is dead ;—whate'er the future bring
    We still can jest, or curse, or laugh, or sing,—
  Though, now and then, impatient words be spoken,
    At least we will not weep.

We will not weep, though hearts be torn and bleeding
  With sorrow for the world's great load of pain,
    At sight of trembling lips and staring eyes,
    Mad faces, bosoms quivering with sighs,—
  And though we hear the piteous voices pleading
    Against their lot in vain.

How would our weeping aid some weary brother,
  Hopeless and joyless as he sweats and delves?
    The tale that man's dark history has told
    May make our pulses throb, our blood run cold,
  But what have we to give to one another
    Who cannot help ourselves ?

We plant our steps in darkness, never knowing
  What Time may carry in its teeming womb ;
    Our best endeavour is to walk erect,
    With hearts no craven terror can affect,
And, scornful of whatever wind is blowing,
  Fearless to wait our doom.

The hour creeps on. We raise our heads, and,
      crossing
  The frozen turf, with lagging steps we roam
    Beneath the blackened trees towards the gate,
    Through which, like thunder of a Highland spate,
We hear the city's restless current tossing
  Its crown of human foam.

The surging waves engulph us in their passage,
  Sweeping us on from sound and sight and ken ;
    But, in the midst of their relentless roar,
    There seem to reach us from a far-off shore
Faint, ghost-like echoes of that ancient message,—
  Peace and goodwill to men.

A REMINISCENCE.

I WONDER if you quite forget
  That summer scene you watched with me,—
The boats with snowy canvas set,
  That moved across the sun-lit sea,—
The houses on the distant hill
  That showed so clear against the sky,—
While stately gulls, with voices shrill,
  In graceful motion glided by.

We rested near the cliff's dark brow,
  And talked of things of every day,—
Mere idle topics that the plough
  Of Time turns up beside the way.
Our voices took no tender tone
  To fan the flaming thoughts aglow,
Save when they mingled with the moan
  That reached us from the waves below.

Our paths since then have seldom crossed ;
  We meet to find old fancies fled ;
And half our younger hopes are lost,
  And half our early friendships dead ;
Yet something of the broken chain
  Is treasured in remembrance yet ;
And still, when summer comes again,
  I wonder if you quite forget.

THROUGH 'THE POOL.'

OUR vessel slips by the anchored ships,
 And the wharves which line the shore,
That is all alive with a human hive,
 And a city's endless roar.
Murky and dun beneath the sun,
 A smoke-cloud veils the light,
As low in the west, like a bird to her nest,
 It sinks to the land of night.
But a gentle breeze is blowing
 The breath of the distant sea,
And the sunlight still is glowing,
 And the river rolling free ;
And the shapes of gloomy buildings
 In the twilight soften down,
Till we skirt the strand of a fairy land
 As we make for London town.

We seem to float in a golden boat
 On a purple and silver stream,
Where the wavelets curl to a crest of pearl
 Round lilies that droop and dream ;
The grimy shore is green once more,
 Like meadows beneath the rain,
And melodies break from the echoes, awake
 To the song of the birds again.

The whispering wind is laden
  With flowery odours rare,
And the voice of a ghostly maiden,
  Who tosses her scented hair ;
The earth is a queen of beauty,
  With the sky for a crimson crown ;
And our souls lie deep in a magic sleep,
  As we make for London town.

LIGHT.

LADY, the world is growing old and tired ;
  We darkly wander in the blinding haze ;
Faded the hopes that once our hearts inspired,
  Feeble the faith that cheered our younger days.
Yet round our bark, amidst the shadows drifting,
  Faint gleams of vanished hours a moment shine,
When, through the clouds and vapours slowly lifting,
  Lady, we gaze upon a face like thine !

Under those brows, that bend in pensive fashion,
  In the clear waters of thy truthful eyes, —
Where is no stain of sorrow, storm, or passion, —
  The witness of thy pure, sweet spirit lies.
No proud disdain, no syren's soft caressing,
  Sully the picture with their presence there, —
Only a look that brings with it a blessing,
  And leaves the sense of something like a prayer.

FROM MY WINDOW.

A sky of palest saffron hue,
Melting in subtle shades to blue,
With floating clouds of purple-gray
Splashed on it in a careless way,
By Nature's brush, the living wind,
With which she moulds them to her mind,

But, woman-like, she scarcely knows
The course in which her fancy flows,
And so she never lets them rest
Upon her canvas in the west,
But round their edges rubs and scrapes,
And makes them ever-changing shapes.

And still the cloud-flakes shift, and soon
I see the gilded crescent-moon
Cut in the sky a pallid scar,
And, paler still, a single star,
That, like a dying glow-worm, shines
Above a dark green nest of pines.

White moths are flitting round the fern,
And overhead a stately hern
Sails homeward, high above the trees,
From which are borne along the breeze
Bird-melodies that, faint and sweet
Like fairy bugles, sound ' Retreat.'

IN THE CHAPEL AT FARNBOROUGH.

In plain black garb thou kneelest there,
A silent figure, still most fair,
· Spite of the silver in thy hair.

How fast since thou hast shared a throne
The sorrow-laden years have flown !
And now thou waitest here alone.

The crown that graced too short a day,
The little spell of sceptred sway,
Power and pomp have passed away.

But Time, the friend of clod and king,
Has decked thee with a nobler thing,
The crown of sacred suffering.

The censer swings, the Mass is said ;
Still lower sinks that drooping head,
In prayer for thy beloved dead.

Outside I hear the thrushes call ;
The slanting sunbeams round thee fall ;—
May God have mercy on us all.

A SOLILOQUY IN EATON SQUARE.

THE summer sun is shining on the Square,
    And seems to bring a gleam of country gladness
To give the town-bred trees a brighter air,
    And force a smile upon the city's sadness.

It glances down upon a grimy seat,
    On which is stretched the raggedest of creatures,—
Some nameless, homeless haunter of the street,
    With matted hair, and most forbidding features.

He turns his eyes towards me, like a cat
    That views its prey with greedy expectation ;
Then, touching what must once have been a hat,
    Assails me with a whining supplication.

Of course, I pay no heed,—we're always taught
    That beggars do this sort of thing for pleasure ;
Their piteous tales are never worth a thought,
    But just composed to wile away their leisure.

Besides, we know those only starve who shirk
    The toil by Nature's kindly laws directed,
And so the rich, —who die of overwork,—
    To sympathise can scarcely be expected.

Not that I'm rich ;—but, still, I'm one of those
    Who sometimes pass within the sacred portals
Of Mammon's shrine, whose glory always throws
    Its glamour even on such humble mortals.

Combined with some slight difference of birth
  It stamps this beggar here as my inferior ;
Though, if we came to reckon up our worth,
  It might be hard to prove myself superior.

True, I've a cleaner collar round my throat,
  Much better boots, and hands a trifle paler,
A silken necktie, and a decent coat
  (For which I owe my too-confiding tailor).

My mind, moreover, has been made a tomb
  For some dead languages and other knowledge,
Though slight, yet not possessed by those for whom
  Millbank or Portland is the only college.

But when you get beyond the outer shell,
  The bodily and mental clothes that screen us,
To tastes and morals, 'twere perhaps as well
  To draw no strict comparisons between us.

In love of pleasure he's akin to me
  ('Tis not to age alone I owe my wrinkles)—
The difference is one of mere degree
  'Twixt oysters and champagne,—and gin and
    winkles.

But custom fain would make him pass his time
  Engrossed in some laborious employment,
And so what's right in me in him's a crime,—
  To live a life devoted to enjoyment.

In truth we hold, in these commercial days,
  The cheapest sins more wicked than the dearest,—
Of all this crooked world's peculiar ways
  Its social laws are certainly the queerest.

We know the tale that came from Palestine,
   When this old Earth was many ages younger,
Of how the wealthy man was wont to dine,
   Regardless of his poorer neighbour's hunger,

And how they died, and changes came about,
   Which quite transformed their relative positions;—
But we've discovered, in this age of doubt,
   The folly of these obsolete traditions.

'Tis true we go to church, which might seem odd,
   But then we do it out of condescension,
Thinking to pay a compliment to God
   By showing Him this delicate attention.

We really cannot bend beneath the yoke
   That lay so heavy on those early sages;—
It might have done for Hebrew fisher-folk,
   But not for us,—'the heirs of all the ages.'

And further, if, like sentimental fools,
   We give to every beggar who importunes,
Regardless of all economic rules,
   How can we ever hope to make our fortunes?

Yet if we fail in that we shall commit
   The only sin that's never now forgiven;
For money is our God, and wanting it
   We cannot get within the modern Heaven.

And yet, from sheer perversity, I think
   I'll give this wretched wanderer a shilling,
And bid him go and get himself a drink,—
   To follow which advice he's not unwilling.

C

You see that from the proper path I've swerved,
  But circumstances strangely alter cases,
And, if we only got what we deserved,
  Our lines would lie in most unpleasant places.

And, as for all your economic stuff,
  I'm willing to admit there's something in it,
But Nemesis is coming soon enough,
  We may as well enjoy the passing minute.

Each of us has his sword of Damocles,—
  Mine is the gout, his the policeman's truncheon ;
So, weary of such well-worn themes as these,
  I'll leave philosophy,—and go to luncheon.

THE LOSING SIDE.

HELMET and plume and sabre, banner and lance and
    shield,
Scattered in sad confusion over the trampled field ;
And a band of broken soldiers, with a weary, hopeless
    air,
With heads in silence drooping and eyes of grim
    despair.
      Like foam-flakes left on the shifting sand,
        In the track of the falling tide,
      On the ground where their cause has failed they
        stand,
        The last of the losing side.

Wisdom of age is vanquished, and generous hopes of
    youth,
Passion of faith and honour, fire of love and truth ;
And the plans that seemed the fairest in the fight
    have not prevailed,
The keenest blades are broken, and the strongest
    arms have failed.
      But souls that know not the breath of shame,
        And tongues that have never lied,
      And the truest hearts, and the fairest fame,
        Are here,—on the losing side.

The conqueror's crown of glory is set with many a
    gem,
But I join not in their triumph,—there are plenty to
    shout for *them.*
The cause is the most applauded whose warriors gain
    the day.
And the world's best smiles are given to the victors
    in the fray.
      But dearer to me is the darkened plain,
        Where the noblest dreams have died,
      Where hopes have been shattered and heroes
        slain
      In the ranks of the losing side.

PLAYED OUT.

WE thought we'd like to play at love,
  And fanned the feeble flame,
But now we find the pastime prove
  A somewhat silly game.

We tried to think it destiny,
  And talked of cruel fate,
And sighed for that which could not be
  Since we had met too late.

A web of passion, fierce and true,
  Our minds were wont to weave,
And all the time we really knew
  'Twas only make-believe.

And thus we saw begin to rise
  A tree without a root,
And feigned to look with longing eyes
  On the forbidden fruit.

But now we see the withered trunk,
  And green leaves turned to dun,
And fallen fruit that, scorched and shrunk,
  Lies rotting in the sun.

It pleases us to play such parts,
  But Nature intervenes,
The interest slackens when our hearts
  Are left behind the scenes.

And, after all, we're forced to own
  No ghost can satisfy
A bosom that has once been shown
  The things which do not die.

We cannot feed the flame that's cold,
  Or man the ruined fort,
And even now the days are old
  For all such empty sport.

And so, like idle girls and boys
  That weary of their play,
We pack them up,—our broken toys,—
  And put the box away.

WHEN AUTUMN WAS THERE.

My thoughts are borne away
  To the shadow of yonder hills,
Where my memory dwells on a strange, sweet day,
  And a vision that time ne'er kills ;
All the doubt and desire and grief of it,
All the hope and delight and belief of it,
  Woven in dreams so fair,
For we fought through the worst of the strife, my
    Love,
And we learned all the meaning of life, my Love,
  When autumn was there.

So little but quickly dies
  In this sad, false world of ours,
And the light will surely change in your eyes,
  As the colours fade from the flowers ;
Though we hold it now, nor care for the cost of it,
Soon, too soon, will the splendour be lost of it,
  Leaving the old despair ;
But our hearts will ne'er be the same, my Love,
As they were e'er they passed through the flame, my
    Love,
  When autumn was there.

THE FUTURE.

It seems so wrong to think of you
  As growing old ;
I scarcely count the story true
  That time has told,
How faces, once as young and fair,
  Have lost their bloom,
How destiny will never spare
One little life, but all must share
  The common doom.

I would that I might hold away
  The hand of fate ;
And yet my heart could scarcely pay
  A price so great !
For soon the load of years would lie
  Upon my brow,
And you would still be young when I
Grew old, and so the love would die
  That links us now.

SILENCE AND SONG.

I MAKE no song to thee,
Save when the lighter fancies of my mind
Play round thy name melodious, as the wind
   Whispers among the leaves of some fair tree ;
And words, like mirthful kisses, may caress
The theme of thine unchanging loveliness,
Though there is nothing they can thus express
   Of what thou art to me.

If I could steal the fire
Of all the poets that have ever sung,—
If harps that by the greatest hands were strung
   Could lend their lofty music to my lyre,—
If thus my song could rise with no restraint
Till the world's voices in its sound grew faint,—
Yet would I never strive in words to paint
   The thoughts thou dost inspire.

Others may choose to sing
Their little loves in modulated tones,—
Just as the brook that tinkles on the stones
   Proclaims itself to be a shallow thing ;
But, as the deeper streams in silence flow,
And hide their ceaseless turmoil far below,
My life's whole current, not my voice, shall show
   What love to thee I bring.

A MODERN PARTING.

AFTER such years of danger and sorrow and hope,
    Of stormy triumph and calm, unwavering bliss,
After spinning each strand in the long laborious rope,
    After climbing the mountain crest,—shall it come to
      this ?

To look at the broken link with a careless eye,
    Where the stealthy rust has bitten right through the
      chain ;
To drop the corroded ends with the scornful sigh
    Of hearts so tired that parting is scarcely pain !

Though their life has quivered and glowed in a single
    fire,
    Blood leaping to blood, and breath awakening
      breath,
Though the bosoms that held them ached with a long
    desire,
    They can leave it without one tear to this living
      death.

Not a kiss,—not a word,—but the touch of an icy hand,
    And the shake of a frozen smile upon trembling lips,
And the flicker of eyes, like the last faint gleam from
    land,
    That darkens behind the waves as the vessel dips.

Oh, God ! is the heart of the world so worn and old
    That the power of passion can fade like a sinking
        star,
That the fever and flush of a life can so soon be cold,
    And the stab in a human spirit can leave no scar ?

It were something still if the burden were sad to bear,
    If the soul were braced for defiance of flame and
        steel, —
There are victories won from the strength of a great
    despair ;
    But what can be gained by the bosoms that hardly
    feel ?

No lurid light on the path of the vanished sun,
    No thunder of storm-swept forests that reel and fall,
But dead leaves dropped in the silence, one by one,
    And the damp cold mist and the darkness over all.

VALE !

KILLED in the morning ! Bear him from the field,
  Though the long battle is but just begun ;
Lay the young soldier on his useless shield,
  And leave the broken sword,—its work is done.

No time for weeping,—scarcely time to sigh ;
  Spread the dark cloak across the pale, fixed face ;
Stand back in silence as it passes by ;
  Then close the ranks,—another take his place.

We must fight on, nor waste in idle tears
  The strength that should sustain us to the end ;
We need the voices he no longer hears
  To shout defiance,—not to mourn our friend.

Short space, at most, the flying moments last ;
  For each and all Time hastens on the track ;
Let night enfold him since his day is past ;
  We follow soon ;—we cannot call him back.

And, after all, his fate may be the best,—
  So early taken from the joyless strife ;
Changing, perhaps, for long, untroubled rest
  The strange delirium that men call ' life.'

And yet it seems a little hard to turn
  Our thoughts away, and leave him lying there.
Eyes will grow wet, and aching bosoms yearn
  To sob a farewell word, or breathe a prayer.

Oh, friend !—if, through the veil that checks our sight,
  Our hearts are now laid open to your gaze,
I do not doubt that you will read aright
  Thoughts that perhaps are shaped in faulty ways.

I do not fear lest you should be deceived
  By words, emotion's most unworthy dress.
I know my heart's design will be believed,
  Which I so vainly struggle to express.

LOW TIDE.

TEARS of the city !—mingled in the stream
  Through long dark banks of mud-bound shingle
    flowing,—
A pallid mirror that reflects the gleam
  Of lurid lamps on anchored barges glowing.
      River of pain !
      Over thee in vain
The ranks of flaring gaslight leer for miles,
      Sad as the lies
      In weary women's eyes,
Flaunting beneath them with their faded smiles.
Love, lust, and anger,—hatred, pain, and hope,—
  Flock to thy shores when earth and sky are sleeping;
Life's varied shapes along thy margin grope,
  And keep thy course replenished with their weeping.

Smiles of the city !—flashing from the moon,
  Whose gold flakes quiver on the dancing waters,—
Blot out the tears, and let thy splendour soon
  Beat on the faces of thy sons and daughters !
      Pierce the dark cloud
      Hanging like a shroud
Over the coffin of their buried joy !
      And as it lifts
      Show them all thy gifts,—
Dreams that are true ; delights that do not cloy !
Smile !—still keep smiling, with the blessed mirth
  So far above thy fevered, loveless laughter,—
So distant from the revelry of earth,
  That leaves but aching heads and bosoms after !

Sighs of the city !—echoed in the wind
  Which stirs the dust upon the footworn pavement,—
Wrung by the hidden grief concealed behind
    The smiling eyes that mock their own enslavement.
        Poor, feeble breath,
        Spared in scorn by Death,
  Who haunts unceasingly beneath the smoke,
        Passage and court
        In which he seeks his sport,
  And chuckles grimly at his hideous joke.
Whispering message of the lips whose prayer,
  Curse, jest, or laughter, leaves the words unspoken
Of anguish borne by those that never dare
    To tell the world of spirits it has broken.

Heart of the city !—throbbing in the beat
  Of endless footsteps that thou canst not number,—
Thy pulse reverberates in every street,
    Nor grants the brief oblivion of slumber.
        What is thy life ?
        Misery and strife,—
  Useless endurance,—labour run to waste,—
        Hopes that are killed,—
        Visions unfulfilled,—
  Fruit fiercely plucked, and bitter to thy taste !
Here, in Time's bark, upon a troubled sea,
  Thy purpose beckons thee for ever shoreward ;
But, though thy million arms are rowing thee,
    Where are the signs that thou art moving forward ?

FALSE REALISM.

THIS, then, is all that you can see in life ?—
      A hopeless struggle,
A maze of wasted effort, useless strife,
      And hideous juggle ;

Where passions rage, without a will to guide,
      In fierce confusion,
And faith, evolved from ignorance and pride,
      Is mere delusion.

Man is a beast, and in his every act
      Most clearly shows it ;
Conscienceless, blind—and yet the strangest fact
      Is that he knows it.

This is the purport of your noble creed !
      This the grand message
That you can offer to the world you've freed,
      Strewn with the wreckage

Of those old legends which you sweep away,
      Fast as you're able,
Leaving your fellows to pursue their way
      Without one fable,

One foolish fancy of those early times
    That owned a duty,
And found in noble dreams as well as crimes
    A spark of beauty.

Ah !—though you beckon us, we stand aloof,
    Breathing defiance.
We will not take your version of the proof
    Offered by Science.

Though bright imaginings should take the shape
    Of foulest matter ;
Though we must suffer our ancestral ape
    To grin and chatter ;

Yet will we fling you back your fiercest scorn,
    Till your lips falter ;
Put back the veil your filthy hands have torn
    Over the altar ;

Draw the sharp sword, and throw away the sheath,
    Peril inviting ;
Cast one last look around, then set our teeth,
    And so die fighting.

What can you tell us that we do not know,
    To prove your theory ?
We want no fresh experience to show
    That life is dreary.

We, too, have suffered and despaired, and lain
    Deep in the mire ;
Felt all our purest aspirations slain
    By dark desire ;

Seen the great temple that our faith had built
    Ruined and shattered ;
Wept for our early innocence, by guilt
    Foully bespattered.

Yet, though we stand with you upon the road,
    Bound for perdition,
With no glad hope to help us bear our load,
    No pure ambition ;

Lost in the weary wilderness of grief ;
    Destined to madness ;
Owning no God, no worship, no belief,
    Save in our sadness ;

Though all our life should only show the flaw
    In our professions ;
Though we should never recognise the law
    Save by transgressions ;

We will not cease to say you lie !—you lie !—
    Spite of your laughter,
We'll ne'er acknowledge that the truth can die
    Here or hereafter.

By the bright visions that we yet can see,
    Through all our blindness ;
By the coarse natures that still bend the knee
    To human kindness ;

By the pure gladness of a maiden's eyes ;
    By the sweet faces
Where that unsullied love which never dies
    Still leaves its traces ;

We feel that all your views of life are wrong,
    Poisonous, rotten ;
Destined to vanish from our thoughts ere long,
    Lost and forgotten.

This is the sole solution we can find ;—
    All that is real
Comes from the misty kingdom of the mind,
    Purely ideal.

RECKONINGS.

Down the dark road on which our souls have
    wandered,
  Halted awhile, we turn our idle gaze,
  Watching the silent ghosts of buried days,
Counting the tracks of time, so lightly squandered.

Not in a bitter mood of useless sorrow
  For the dead joys we cannot call to life ;
  But in some brief cessation of the strife,
Ere we take breath, and turn to face the morrow.

Then, with the calm, unclouded eye of reason,
  We see the distance covered, and the cost
  Of present gain in that which we have lost,
And balance debt and credit for a season.

Cold and impartial, with a glance we measure
  The stock of solid merchandise we hold,
  The store of commonplace, commercial gold,—
But not imagination's cherished treasure.

Setting aside our Youth's romantic vision,
  We write the sum of profit still unspent,—
  Comfort, self-satisfaction, peace, content,—
Testing their worth with strictest supervision.

And we perceive how these have only flourished
   In the seclusion we too seldom sought ;
   In the cool shade of quiet work and thought ;
By stern restraint and strict obedience nourished ;

Far from the clamour of unanswered questions ;
   Far from the warrior's defiant shout ;
   Far from the whisperings of chilly doubt ;
Far from our climbing Fancy's wild suggestions ;

Not in the lurid atmosphere of passion,
   Forced into growth by burning hopes and fears,
   Scorched by our breath, and blistered by our tears;—
But gently nurtured in a simpler fashion,

By the soft cherishing of friends,—not lovers ;
   In smiling gardens,—not on battle-fields ;
   Not by the forces proud ambition wields,
But by the spell that sympathy discovers.

In sheltered English homes ; in sun-kissed meadows ;
   In autumn woods, when leaves are turning brown ;
   In sleepy stillness of some grey-walled town ;
Peace makes her nest, half hid by life's dim shadows.

Thus Reason reckons ; but, in fierce resistance,
   Impulses rise her verdict to withstand,
   Snatch the half-finished figures from her hand,
And cry, That is not life, but mere existence !

How can he conquer who has shunned the battle ?
   How can he climb who greatly fears to fall ?
   How can he hope to hear the trumpet-call
Whose ears are drinking in the streamlet's prattle ?

Better to face our lot, however dire !
  Better to speak, though none should choose to hear !
  Better to live, though death might silence fear !
Better to fight, though cowards bid retire !

Better to love, and feel the flame of Heaven,
  Though it should brand us with a lasting scar !
  Better to follow Truth's resistless car,
Though through the blackest Hell it may be driven !

Talk not of peace !   'Twere nobler far to spurn it
  While the strife rages !   If there should be peace
  When our blind struggles here at last shall cease,
Those who have dared to fight must surely earn it !

CLEANTHES IN OUR DAYS.

THOU, that our eyes cannot see, that our thoughts
    cannot paint,
Thy form and Thy nature are pictured by prophet
    and saint;
But none can interpret a vision so vague and so faint.

Though we labour and listen and learn, we are granted
    no part
In knowledge that is not of Earth,—yet there glow in
    man's heart
Sparks that Earth never has lit; and we know that
    Thou art.

Once we believed that Thy shrine and Thine altar
    must be
Far from the turmoil of men, and our hearts cried to
    Thee
On some loneliest peak of the land,—in some depth of
    of the sea.

We thought that Thou never couldst dwell in the
    strife that we saw
So close on Man's footsteps; we thought that the
    code of Thy law
Must be written on pages less spotted with blemish
    and flaw.

We thought we could see Thy design in the forests
    that grew
On dark mountain-sides; in the meadows that flashed
    with Thy dew;
In the tremulous grass; in the flowers that blossomed
    anew;

In the glades that had darkened their green in the
    soft summer rain;
In the mist-shrouded river that stole through the
    slumbering plain;
In the sunset that reddened the sky, with the stars in
    its train.

We thought that Thy voice only spoke in the hurri-
    cane's roar;
In the whisper of leaves; in the song feathered throats
    would outpour;
In the thunderbolt's crash; in the sob of the waves
    on the shore.

But now Thou hast guided our steps, till at last we
    are brought
To discern by what various methods Thy lessons are
    taught,
And, leaving the sphere of emotion, we seek Thee in
    thought.

Though melodies sink for a while in the silence of
    night,
And we strive from the harp-strings to get but the
    harmonies right,
In time Thou wilt blend them in strains of the purest
    delight.

Though it darken the meaning of much in the pages
    we scan,
Though it weaken the light that we fancied was thrown
    on Thy plan,
No longer we count upon Nature complete without
    Man.

Man, who has stumbled and toiled through such
    sorrowful years ;
Man, with his passions and efforts, his hopes and his
    fears ;
Man, with his scorn and his worship, his laughter and
    tears.

Now the vast scope of Thy purpose begins to be
    shown ;
Nothing is wasted ; throughout hast Thou made it
    Thine own ;
Nothing is common or worthless, for all is Thy
    throne.

Fruits, sweet and bitter, Thou givest, on which Man
    may sup ;—
All have been grown in Thy field ; Thou wilt gather
    them up
At harvest, and press the red juices out into Thy
    cup.

Fruit of our blunders and blindness, our pain and our
    strife ;
Fruit of our labour and yearning, with failure so
    rife ;
Fruit of the trees that have stood in the garden of
    life.

Surely the follies and faults which Thy purpose have
    crossed
Shall count but as steps in the dark, shall be held but
    the cost
Of attainment, and all shall be gathered, and none
    shall be lost.

The sword that the soldier has brandished, the dart
    he has flung,
The speech that the statesman has tossed from his
    fiery tongue,
The song that the feverish lips of the poet have sung,

All hopes, all desires, all dreams, every guerdon and
    goal
Man strives for and aims at so blindly, are part of one
    whole,
And Thou wilt interpret the riddles—Thou infinite
    Soul !

And Action and Knowledge and Art as Religion shall
    prove ;
And Virtue and Beauty and Truth shall be blended in
    Love ;—
Love, the pure breath of Thy life that Thou breathest
    above ;

Love, the great measureless mountain, that lifts on its
    brow
What has been—what shall be—what is—in a limit-
    less Now ;—
Love the ineffable mystery ;—Love that is Thou.

QUESTIONS.

ENDLESS questions !—Why are we here
    Forced to go on whate'er betide,
With the dimmest of lights by which to steer,
    And dangers waiting on every side ?
        Why must we toil
        On a barren soil,
    Fettered and cramped by a load of chains,
        Held by a breath
        Betwixt life and death ?—
What does it matter ?—the fact remains.

Endless riddles of fear and doubt !
    Is there a Heaven ?—Is there a Hell ?
Where shall we be when the sand runs out ?
    How will our lives look ?—ill or well ?
        In a future vast
        Will the spectres last
    Of feeble purpose and broken vow ?
        Is it foul or fair
        In the shadows there ?
What does it matter ?—we're here just now.

Better to scramble on and strive
  To get what laughter and love we can,
To keep a glimmer of hope alive,
    And a kindly thought for our brother man.
      Shallow, indeed,
      You may call the creed,
Yet a straw to clutch is a priceless boon.
      There are trials enough,
      And the road is rough ;—
But what does it matter ?—it ends so soon.

TO THE OLD GODS.

BROWN leafage clear against the blue
    Of yonder stainless Autumn sky,
Washed by the liquid sunbeams turns to gold,
    And pale mists lie
Like gossamer across the woodland breast
Of each enchanted hill, whose tree-clad crest
Forms in the dancing rays a picture new,
    Though every line be old.

Oh ye who dwell in haunted glade,
    Dew-crystalled slope, and sounding stream,—
Whose voices have been known, since time began,
    To all that dream
Of things no brain can fathom, when they hear
The magic mountain echoes calling clear,—
Bring back the deathless vision once displayed
    To weary, toiling man !

No taint of useless discontent
    Moves me to murmur and repine
Because the stream of change is never still,
    Strong faith is mine
That, though the world outwears its ancient dress,
There lives beneath its smoke-strained duskiness
A beauty, which no art can supplement,
    No earthly change can kill.

But though it be our boast to look
    Under the illusory disguise
To which that spirit now doth condescend,
    And though our eyes
No longer need the sunlight to translate
The riddles stamped upon the scroll of Fate,
We do not find the meaning of the book
    So plain as we pretend.

We tune our fancy to the pitch
    Of all those complex harmonies
By which the apparent discords are redeemed ;
    Strange melodies
Speak to us softly through the brazen din
Of modern anguish, and our hearts begin
To gather priceless ore from veins of which
    Our fathers never dreamed.

But—as the war-stained victor's breast
    Yearned for his plough-land's simple peace
Far from the triumphs of applauding Rome,—
    We cannot cease
To love the scanty moments when we view
Those half-imagined mountains, faint and blue,
Under whose shade our old illusions rest,
    Our dreams have found a home.

We build our comfort on the thought
    That all this endless birth and death
Is but the strenuous progress of our race,
    Gasping for breath
With slow, laborious effort, as it plants
Its footsteps on the road which upward slants,—
That each ensuing agony has bought
    A somewhat higher place.

The rough old school of stormy deeds,
Whose mark was branded on the life
Of other generations, has been lost ;
      And mental strife
A tribute from our passions fiercely claims,—
The lust of wealth,—the sordid social aims,—
The fret and fever of conflicting creeds ;
      Has it been worth the cost ?

I fear my heart is out of tune
When all these jarring voices throb ;
I cannot join in the triumphant psalm
      Whereby the mob
Proclaims its rising strength, nor can I share
The vain regrets of cowards who despair,
Watching the waves with floating wreckage strewn
      When tempest yields to calm.

The news opposing preachers tell
Rings empty to my doubting ears,—
I cannot gauge each rival system's worth ;
      The bitter tears,
The reckless laughter of humanity
Are shrouded in such unknown mystery,—
I think we pass through Heaven and through Hell
      Here, in our life on Earth.

I have no part with those who bend
In contemplation o'er the brink
Of depths where science pours her dusky streams,—
      Nor do I think
Artistic shiboleths and cultured cant
Sufficient for the tired combatant,
Who looks to find life's greatest aim and end
      In action,—not in dreams.

My soul doth not aspire to prove
Some problem, such as those which vex
Cold, prurient professors of the lore
    That deals with sex ;
I would not weigh desire, nor analyse
The worth of stormy bosoms, flaming eyes ;—
I take my lesson from the lips of love,
    And ask to learn no more.

Oh for some feeling, good or bad,
    To tear the smooth, complacent mask
Through which the world serene and senseless grins,—
    With no great task
To rouse its drooping powers,—no dim ideal
To scourge it into doing something real,—
With soulless sloth and dull convention clad,
    Whether it strives or sins !

Forgotten deities !—I turn
    To hide amidst your woods and rocks
My passionate, rebellious, home-sick heart ;—
    Unorthodox,
Unshrinking, unrepentant,—proud to be
Despised of worshippers that bend the knee
To false, new gods, whose shallow cult I spurn,
    Choosing to walk apart.

Grant me a glimpse of fairyland
    Here in your garden !—let me leave
All haunting memories outside the gate !
    Fain would I weave
Dream-pictures in the shadows, and forget
The load of thought, the burden of regret ;
Shroud me with mist !—I do not understand,—
    I am content to wait.

SUNSHINE.

A BREEZY, quivering summer day ;
   Light on the heather and furze and fern ;
Light on the dancing leaves that play
   At ballroom tricks as they bend and turn.

A face that never has known a frown ;
   A graceful figure,—a dainty dress ;
Eyes and hair of the blackest brown ;
   And a glance of laughing friendliness.

Lightly goes, as it lightly came,
   The glimmer that broke through the cloudy strife,
And the grim old landscape is just the same—
   Save a little green spot on the sands of life.

E

FROM A TRAVELLING ACQUAINT-ANCE.

I⊤ was chance that brought you across my life,
  As you blundered on in the painful track,
When your heart was sick with the useless strife,
  And your eyes were weary of looking back.
You were faint with the toil and the dust and heat,
  When you saw how I stood here watching you,
And you wanted to rest your tired feet,
  So you stopped to talk,—as travellers do.

Well ! we have talked,—and the time slips on,
  And the long straight road is before you still ;
'Twere a pity to wait till the day be gone
  Ere you cross the valley and climb the hill.
Yet you seem as though you were half-inclined
  To loiter a little and hesitate,—
As though you could scarcely know your mind,
  And were trying your strength for a fight with Fate.

For you cast a restless glance around
  On the fair green turf beside the stream,
Where the water glides with a soothing sound,
  And the May-flies dance, and the lilies dream ;
And you turn to ask me, half in jest,
  If the dreary struggle is worth the cost,
If it were not better to wait and rest
  On the shady spot that your path has crossed,

Where voices call you from out the wood,
    And the fruit hangs ripe on the bending boughs,—
For you seem to have gained so little good
    From your younger hopes and your early vows.
And you doubt if it pays to dedicate
    The toil of your life to a high intent,—
It were easy to pause, ere it grow too late,
    And enjoy the gifts that the gods have sent.

Oh, my friend !—if my words have any force,
    If you value the poor advice you ask,
I beseech you to tread the appointed course,
    To attain the goal and complete the task.
For you know that the voices are not true,
    There are deadly mists on the river shore,
And the fruit, so golden and fair to view,
    Is rotten and poisonous at the core.

Keep on !—Though the goal be out of sight,
    You may find it yet on a distant day,
When the clouds shall break, and the wrong come
        right,
    And the doubt and the gloom be swept away.
Though your spirit has still so much to bear,
    There is strength to sustain, and hope to bless,—
Be it only the strength of a stern despair,
    And the hope of an utter hopelessness.

Who am I,—you will say,—that I should preach
    These lofty aims which I ne'er pursue ?
For I do not practise the truth I teach,
    Nor follow the path that I point to you.

Ah !—the question brings its own reply—
  I know too well what these things are worth—
I have paid for my knowledge, and that is why
  I would guide your footsteps to firmer earth.

If you do as I ask your choice may bring
  Still greater results than you now can see,
For the pendulum has a backward swing;
  And in saving yourself you may succour me.
There is many a link on the chain of time
  That may fetter our lives though we do not know,
That may tighten its grip on the souls that climb,
  And tie them to those that are left below.

And the strange old legend may yet be right
  Of a God Who will sit on the Judgment Seat,
And drag all the doubtful past to light,
  As we kneel there naked before His feet.
And you, who have won, shall abide the test
  Unscathed, ere you pass to your place in Heaven,
While we, who have failed, can only rest
  On our piteous prayer to be forgiven.

And then you can raise your voice for me,
  And say how I tried to help you now,
How I broke the brambles, and set you free,
  And washed the stains from your bleeding brow ;
How I held you back from the fatal brink,
  And stirred your courage, and bid you mount,
When you almost had set your mind to sink ;—
  And it may be that God will let it count,

DEJECTION.

THE wild, bleak common slopes away
  To meet the line of smoky mist,
  The spectre that has stooped and kissed
With chilly breath the sombre clay,
  And dared the daylight to resist
The pressure of its ghostly hand
Which kills the colours of the land,
  And turns the green to gray.

Black on the distant uplands lie
  The woods that own no living leaf,
  But, clustering in dim relief
Against the changeless leaden sky,
  Still wear the threadbare garb of grief,
As though they ne'er could cease to mourn
Who saw the pallid Frost-king born,
  And watched the summer die.

Faded the grass beneath my feet !
  Faded the heart within my breast !
  And, in its saddest garments dressed,
My mind has wandered forth to meet
  The blighting spirit that has pressed
Upon the childhood of the year,
And turned its smile into a sneer,
  And soured all its sweet.

THE IDOL.

Said the poet, 'Who is this that I have followed
    through the night?
      Is it she whom I would love,
        The spirit not of Earth?
      I have prayed the gods above
        To grant celestial birth
To the soul that shall make perfect my life and my
    delight,
      That shall quench the fierce desire
      Which has ravaged with its fire
All the harvest of my heart, and left a dearth.

'I have weighed, and found them wanting, the
    daughters of mankind.
      In the garden where they stray
        I can hear the serpent hiss;
      And their passion dies away
        In the phantom of a kiss.
I know that I must search beyond the beaten tracks
    to find
      The prize that I have sighed for,
      That the noblest hearts have died for,—
The gem that mortals seek and ever miss.

' But now mine eyes have seen her in the silver of the
dawn.
By the pearly light I trace
Her footsteps in the dew,
Though the mist had dimmed her face,
Yet my throbbing bosom knew
Who it was that swiftly passed o'er the daisy-
sprinkled lawn.
'Twas for her my spirit panted,
And the gods my prayer have granted ;—
I will follow now, and prove the vision true.

As he spoke, the sun climbed up o'er the mountain's
rosy rim ;
And it flooded all the vale
In a sea of liquid light.
But the poet's face grew pale,
For, before his troubled sight,
Was a faulty, mortal woman, who stood and smiled at
him.
And the scornful gods laughed proudly,
As his voice assailed them loudly,—
' Put out the sun, and give me back the night !'

WANDERERS.

We followed the path of years,
  And walked for a while together
Through the hills of hope and the vale of fears,
Sunned by laughter, and washed by tears,
  In the best and the worst of weather.

Till we came to a gloomy wood,
  Where our steps were forced asunder
By the twisted, tangled trees that stood,
Meeting above like a frowning hood,
  With a world of darkness under.

And whenever by chance we met
  In the woodland's open spaces,
We were bruised and tattered and soiled and wet,
With much to pity,—forgive,—forget,
  In our scarred and dusty faces.

Well !—it was long ago,
  And the leaves in the wood are falling,
As we wander wearily too and fro,
With many a change in our hearts I know,—
  But still I can hear you calling.

THE GIFT OF SPRING.

I AND my horse alone
    In the depth of a leafless lane,
Where the thick brown buds have shown
    That the green is coming again,
    And soft, bright patches are plain,
Where the leaves are beginning to peep.
And the great Earth-spirit at last is breaking
The chains with whose load it has long been aching,
And stretching its stiffened limbs, and waking
    From its sleep.

Slowly we pass along,
    And my heart cries out at the sound
Of the thrilling, turbulent song
    From the larks which quiver around,
    Far up from the sun-kissed ground,
On the breast of the still, blue sky,
Like fishermen's boats on a calm sea riding,
And, as if aroused by their mirthful chiding,
An army of birds, in the thickets hiding,
    Makes reply.

Wandering over a field
    Mine eyes unguided fall
On a red house, half-concealed
    By the ivy on every wall,
    And the bushes, so dense and tall

That they scarce show more than the roof,
As they stand around in the quiet garden,
And shut out the stranger's gaze, and harden
Their hearts against him, nor ask his pardon
    For reproof.

    I have no wish to look
      Where the gold of a neighbour lies,
    Or to turn the leaves of a book
      Never written for careless eyes,
      But a vague desire will rise
To know how the world may seem
To the hearts that in yonder house are beating,
And I breathe them the thought of a kindly greeting,
As watermen hail, for a moment meeting
    On a stream.

    Late on a night in June,
      As you pass through a lamp-lit street,
    The wail of a throbbing tune
      And the shuffle of dancers' feet
      May float through a window, and beat
Like a pulse in your listening ears,
And open the door of remembrance, bringing
Faint echoes of long-dead voices, ringing
With music of laughter, and sighing, and singing,
    And of tears.

    Now is a kindred spell
      On my dreaming senses cast,
    Till my fancy seems to dwell
      In the twilight vague and vast
      Of a formless, shadowy past,

And a time that was never real,
When life was in wondering more than in doing,
When the limit of love was a hazy wooing,
And the soul looked up to the stars, pursuing
    An ideal.

    But I turn to face the truth,
      And let the memories go,
    For the phantom visions of youth
      Have slept so long that I know
      It were better to leave them so,
    Than to strive to awaken them yet,
To disturb my soul with their vain intrusion,
And rouse from their slumbers, in wild confusion,
The spectres of many a lost illusion,
    And regret.

    For there is a future still,
      However the past be lost,
    And the gain in knowledge and will
      Has been surely worth the cost ;
      And, when half the desert is crossed,
    It were foolish to halt and play
With the bones that have lain so long and whitened,
Though they be the relics of forms that have brightened
The darkness at which we have once been frightened
    For a day.

    But future and past are nought
      In the face of a day like this ;
    Sensation is better than thought
      When my heart is aglow with the bliss
      Of a long, delirious kiss

From Nature's passionate mouth,
While her silken lashes are lazily lifting,
And the smile in her eyes is flashing and shifting,
And her languorous breath comes softly drifting
From the south.

So I make for a winding track,
That crosses a lonely heath,
And leave the past at my back,
As the wind blows fresh in my teeth,
And trample the future beneath
The hoofs of my galloping horse,
'Mid the jingle of steel and the groan of leather,
As we swing to his sweeping stride together,
Through a billowy ocean of waving heather
And of gorse.

Old Earth, you have made me quaff
A cup of your rarest wine !
And my spirit begins to laugh
With the joy of that draught divine.
And the treasures of life are mine,
And the pomp and power of Kings,
As the maddening sun of your splendour blazes ;
And my heart pours out the stream of your praises ;—
Though weak and unworthy the voice it raises,
Yet it sings.

THE ENIGMA.

WHAT canst thou give?
Or what the service thou would'st ask of me?
    In the blue waters of thine eyes
    A radiance soft and fugitive
Lights the transparent depths, before it dies
    Like sunbeams on the sea.

    Oh, smiling lips,
And pensive brow beneath the waving hair!—
    How looks the secret thought behind
    When some unguarded moment strips
The veil of polished custom from the mind
    Which moves that face so fair?

    Is life a jest,—
A sun-lit ripple on the stream of Time,
    Whose rainbow course but serves to wake
    Mirthfullest fancies in thy breast,
And never once impels thy thoughts to break
    From comic to sublime?

    Or dost thou feel
The burden of this world's unrestful yoke?
    Perchance thy gentle laughter mocks
    The bitterness thou dost conceal,
Like the young Spartan, when he held the fox
    Gnawing beneath his cloak.

I cannot doubt
That, in the passage of the drifting years,
   Thy cup has sometimes over-brimmed
   With sorrow, freely measured out,
Which choked the music of thy voice, and dimmed
   Those April eyes with tears.

But has it killed
The scented, fragile flowers that I know
   Must surely in such soil have bloomed?
   Has the black breath of winter chilled
Their growth, and left them for thy life-time doomed
   To sleep beneath the snow?

From thy clear brain
The summer-lightning of thy wit doth start,
   In flashes that illuminate
   The darkness of life's barren plain,—
But, though its brilliancy doth ne'er abate,
   How is it with thy heart?

I do but ask
A fruitless question,—thou wilt not unfold
   The eternal riddle of the Sphinx;
   No sight can penetrate the mask
That shields the structure when a woman thinks,—
   The tale is never told.

It is enough
That thou dost turn on me a softened look;
   Hope's candle fitfully has burned
   Because the winds of Fate are rough,
And many a mournful lesson have I learned
   In reading through the book.

But yesterday
The sunbeams cast a pallid, golden hue
    Upon the flag-stones at my feet,
    And wiped the dreary film of gray
From their sad faces, while above the street
    The sky was almost blue.

And in my veins
The blood moved faster than a mountain stream ;
    And soon my troubled spirit broke
    The deadening bondage of its chains,
And passed away beyond the pall of smoke
    Into a misty dream.

I felt the breath
Of slumber-laden breezes from the south ;
    Faint essence of the dewy fields,
    Of damp leaves, vaguely sweet in death,
Calmed me with that soft taste its fragrance yields
    Cool in my fevered mouth.

The drowsy sense
Of harmony and colour in the air
    Seemed for a little while to break
    The force of the desire intense,
The stress of soul with which our bosoms ache,—
    Twin-sister to despair.

The heart doth yearn
With restless hunger for it scarce knows what,—
    And all my nature rose to thank
    This gleam of sunshine, that could turn
My thoughts for one bright moment from the blank
    Of that which cometh not.

But now once more
The sky is like the ceiling of a room
 Discoloured with a cake of dust,—
 The street is haggard as before,
And the distempered, lurid light doth rust
 Brown in the murky gloom.

 And even so
Doth love's bright bubble vanish in a day ;—
 I've seen it by a sunbeam nursed,
 And thought that it would never go,
Till hands have tried to grasp it, and it burst
 Into a shred of spray.

 'Twere vain to dwell
With profitless repining on the past ;—
 Fate binds the broken strands anew ;
 And I will yield me to the spell,
And care not if the dream be false or true,
 So long as it shall last.

 I'll be thy harp,
And thou shalt touch the strings with roving hand ;
 And, though the wanton notes be strewn
 In reckless waste, I will not carp
At any chord, if strange should be the tune,
 And hard to understand.

 Whatever whim
Governs thy mind my spirit shall respond ;
 Fickle or steadfast, true or false,
 In lightest play or purpose grim,
While Fate shall fiddle we will try to valse,
 Nor turn our thoughts beyond.

For life is short,
And man's desire is long as Art itself ;
   And, though the scars be branded deep
   Which show the price of such a sport,
We'll leave the relics of dead dreams to sleep
   On Memory's dusty shelf.

   Oh, deign to be
A harbour from the tempest of my heart !
   Suffer my shattered boat to ride
   Safe from the fury of the sea,
E'en though the turning of to-morrow's tide
   Bid me once more depart.

   If love's a stage
I'll tread it with a foot that falters not ;
   I'll take my part whate'er it means,
   And play it out from page to page,
Nor ever seek to look behind the scenes,
   Nor ask to know the plot.

   Let me but cool
My forehead in the snows of thy soft breast !
   Scatter thy hair across mine eyes !
   I would not now be Passion's fool,
But only wish to calm the voice that cries
   Within my soul for rest.

   Soothe me to sleep !
And let thy kisses quench the burning tears
   With which my weary eye-balls ache !
   The silence of that slumber deep
May charm my swooning senses till it wake
   The music of the spheres.

LIFE'S GAMBLE.

SHUFFLE the cards, and deal them out !
  Gather the gold in lumps !
Whatever your hand, you can scarcely doubt
  That somebody gets the trumps.
What are the stakes we shall play for ?—choose !
  A fortune ?—a name ?—a friend ?
Well—some will win, and the rest will lose,—
  And it's all the same in the end.

If you're beaten, an angry thought will start
  Of the change which might have been
If, in place of a spade, you had held a heart,
  Or an ace instead of a queen,
If you win, you will find that the interest died
  When your luck began to mend,
For never a player is satisfied,—
  And it's all the same in the end.

ART.

In silver flood the moonbeams fall,
　　And paint each sloping buttress white
That bends across the Abbey wall
　　Clear-stamped upon the face of night.

As grief to gladness, hate to love,
　　The contrasts of the picture grow,—
The great eternal calm above,—
　　The stream of gas-lit life below.

Twin-mysteries that none can read,—
　　Questions with answers never found,—
More ancient than the oldest creed,—
　　More modern than the forms around.

No sage's lore, no zealot's prayer,
　　Can make those endless riddles clear,—
The message of the silence there,—
　　The meaning of the turmoil here.

Yet puny man, with scornful lips
　　Pursed to a smile of self-conceit,
Still poses as the bee that sips
　　From every flower the burden sweet.

He dockets this, and labels that,
    Believing, when he learns the cause
Of light and shadow, round and flat,
    His mind alone has made the laws.

He writes a petty code of rules,
    To build or ruin, bless or curse,—
Then gives them to his brother-fools
    As secrets of the universe.

But all unseen the Spirit lies
    To hear him mouth her epitaph,—
Watching, with cold majestic eyes,
    And lips that never deign to laugh.

TO CERTAIN YOUNG GENTLEMEN.

Poor little vapid, useless brood !
  What man would trouble to upbraid you?
'Twas Nature's most sarcastic mood
  In which she made you.

The dandy of a by-gone day,
  Who showed, no doubt, some foolish features,
Would still have made a good display
  Besides such creatures.

The foppish airs of all his school, —
  The flaming coat and waistcoast flowered
Might sometimes serve to grace a fool,
  But not a coward.

For if some rashly spoken word
  Should chance to land him in a quarrel,
He did not shrink from naked sword,
  Or pistol-barrel.

And when the storm-clouds swept the sky,
  And England's fiercest foes assailed her,
He answered to his country's cry,
  Nor ever failed her.

But on a thousand battle-plains,
  When death crept near, he stood and faced it ;
Knowing what blood was in his veins,
  He ne'er disgraced it.

A darker sight would stand revealed
  If, stirred by danger and dejection,
Poor England's trustful voice appealed
  To your protection.

You'd wave aside with polished scorn
  The summons to such vulgar duty,
Too rough for dainty creatures born
  To worship beauty ;—

To plan the texture of a dress
  For sportive dames to flaunt and flirt in ;—
To shade a lamp ;—to match a tress ;—
  Or drape a curtain.

To squirm, and gush, and rhapsodise
  On little arts you dip your tastes in ;—
To scent your hair, and paint your eyes,
  And pinch your waists in ;—

To shudder at the clumsy sports
  Of rude, ungraceful Goths and Vandals ;—
To breath intelligence of courts ;—
  Or whisper scandals ;—

To fritter on from year to year,
  And shrink, as if the contact hurt you,
From all that's manliest in the sphere
  Of vice or virtue.

The sottish clowns, who seethe and stew
    In lust, and blood, and drunken passion,
Defile God's image less than you—
    Bright stars of fashion !

The giant world, whose groaning breast
    Is scorched by flames that never languish,
Still labours on, and finds no rest
    From toil and anguish ;—

Young heads grow white with anxious thought ;
    Strong limbs are bent ; true hearts are tired ;
And human hopes are sold and bought ;
    And brains are hired.

The scornful Fates, serene on high,
    Still brew for man his bitter potion ;—
But you go gaily dancing by,
    Without emotion.

You never touch the draught they mix,—
    For other mouths that cruel cup is ;—
Your task is to perform your tricks,
    Like poodle puppies.

Well,—we are told some good may spring
    From hideous facts that make us tremble,
From many a little crawling thing
    Which you resemble,—

Since Nature suffers you to live,
    In her design she doubtless needs you ;—
We'll hope that Heaven may forgive
    The land that breeds you.

AFTER RAIN.

FLOW, gray river, under the bridge
   That cuts a curve on the opal sky,
Where the dim cloud-mountains, ridge on ridge,
   Crested with rose and saffron lie.
Flow, gray river !—the sunken sun
   Withdraws the folds of its bright day-dress,
And the stars come quivering, one by one,
   To light the path of thy loneliness.

Voices ring in the wind to-night
   As it stirs the shuddering London trees,
And the sad, low tones of their pleading smite
   To the depths of a bosom ill at ease.
Shadowy ghosts from the pavement rise,
   In the garb of memories lost for years,
And search my soul with their pleading eyes
   Flashing to mine through a veil of tears.

AT ST. LUNAIRE.

SEA before me and sky above me, and not one stain
    upon sky or sea,
But the depth of a vast transparent blue, by clouds
    unsullied, from shadows free ;
And the golden blaze of flowering gorse on the cliff's
    green summit above, that kills
The paler fires of primrose tufts, and the duskier
    gleam of the daffodils.

Light and slumber for once have met, with scarce an
    echo from sea or land,
Save the surging murmur where wavelets foam in pure
    white lines on the yellow sand,
Or the cry of a moving seagull flaked on the sky's
    blue ground like a spot of snow,
Or a voice from the field where the ploughman guides
    his labouring oxen to and fro.

Under my feet, like a carpet laid, are countless
    thousands of tiny shells,
Frail as the petals from roses blown, and pink as the
    first young heather bells,
Crisp and dainty like frozen froth, or magic scales by
    the mermaids shed,
Who have slept here once, when the tide was high,
    on the weeds that softened their sandy bed.

Sound of them crushed by my careless motion shoots
    a thought, like a lantern gleam,
Into the fog where my mind endeavours to shape the
    sense of a tangled dream
Of vague repining and feeble hope, and all the flicker-
    ing wants that roll
Their clouds of vapour and tongues of flame through
    the seething gulf of a human soul.

Fancy whispers a soft suggestion, takes these splintered
    shells for a text,
Points a finger of pleasant scorn at the brain with its
    floating troubles vexed,
Painting facts in their true proportion, free from the
    self-esteem which throws
A light unreal on the paltry pain that every earthly
    bosom knows.

What are these boasted lives of ours but flimsy shells
    on the shores of time,
Massed in a helpless multitude in a setting of sand
    and weed and slime,
Scorched and cracked by the burning sun, or caked
    with the salt of the drifting spray,
Left between a tide and a tide for a fraction at most
    of the summer day?

What can it matter if some be broken under the
    twisted heel of chance,—
Reckless demon that cares not whither its footsteps
    turn in the giddy dance?

Soon or late must they all be shattered and swept
    away by the restless sea,
As the turn of the tide sends rolling back the cruel
    breakers of Destiny.

Out of the mists of the buried ages flaunt the spectres
    of human lives,—
Crowded millions that none can number, wandering
    cattle that no man drives ;
Each one bent with a load of sorrow, of pain and
    passion, of wrath and love ;
Mocked by the voices that call beneath, and dazed by
    the pitiless glare above.

Weary heart,—let the red blood beat in thy veins
    unwatered by useless tears !
What art thou in this host whose course is a change-
    less stream through the shifting years?—
Only a flash from the fire of time, that flings so many
    a short-lived spark,
As the lightning leaps from the thunder-cloud, to be
    lost in another as drear and dark.

Ask no more than has now been given,—the power to
    feel and the strength to be,—
The smile of the sun, and the kiss of the breeze, and
    the plaintive song of the moaning sea.
Though the waves returning will grind the shells to
    a shapeless pulp on the tide-swept shore,
They will fashion them into the soil of a land that
    the world is waiting for,—ask no more.

ECHOES.

THERE came a little wild bird and nestled in my
    breast,
    And clung to me and loved me in the days gone by;
It sang to me such music that my soul was lulled to
    rest,
    And this Earth's discordant voices seemed to sink
    and die.

But my feet were doomed to walk upon the dusty side
    of life,
    Where the dingy smoke had turned the sky from
    blue to gray,
And my little bird grew weary of the clamour and the
    strife,
    So mournfully it spread its wings and soared away.

And now I wander lonely in the sombre-coloured
    street
    That re-echoes with the murmur of a restless throng,
Like the throbbing of a sick man's pulse at fever-
    heat;—
    And still I try to whistle them my wild bird's song.

SONNETS.

IRELAND.

OUT of the bosom of the silent deep
  Our vessel came, and moved along the shore,
  Too far to hear the breakers' restless roar,
Yet near enough to see their white arms creep
Up the black rocks that stood there, stern and steep,
  Then tumble backwards at their feet once more ;
  Like living souls, which vainly strive to soar,
And fall, and fail,—and sadly sink to sleep.
And, as I looked on the great lonely hills,
  Shrouded so mournfully in mist and rain,
  With here and there a sun-gleam breaking through,
  It seemed to me as though at last I knew
Why music of this land so strangely thrills,
  And mingles tears with laughter, love with pain.

OXFORD.

WHAT shall I say of thee?—No words can paint
  The strange enchantment by thy beauty cast
  On heart and brain. Dim fancies crowding fast,
Shadowy ghosts, and visions vague and quaint
Break on my senses, with the murmur faint
  Of some dead voice, forgotten in the past,
  Yet wafting fairy echoes to the last
Through these unfaded haunts of sage and saint.

Dream-city, bathed in the soft evening light!
  On tower and roof the dying sunbeams quiver,
Kiss thee to sleep, and leave thee for the night,
  Clasped to the bosom of thine ancient river,
By whose voice lulled thou sinkest to thy rest,
  Like a fair lady on her lover's breast.

MY WISH.

ONE gift I ask, as nearly best of all ;—
   A heart against my hardest fortune steeled,
   A high resolve, which shall oppose its shield
To all the fears that might my soul appal.
Grant me to set my back against the wall ;
   And, whatsoever fate may hold the field,
   Helpless or hopeless, let me never yield,
But wait the stroke, and undefeated fall.

Guerdon of victory I hold most dear ;
   But rather than obtain it in the ways
That suffer influence of any fear,
   I trust that I might scorn the wished-for bays ;—
Not like the reed that bent, but like the oak
   That stood against the storm, and standing broke.

B

SOLITUDE.

LIFE is a sea, where chance has roughly thrown
   A group of scattered islands ; and on each
   There lives a soul which vainly longs for speech
With those that dwell on islands next its own.
The secrets of their life are never shown,
   For sight of straining eyeballs cannot reach
   Beyond the shingle of the distant beach,
And all their inland motions are unknown.

Yet now and then a passing sunbeam rends
   The wall of mist, and for a space they see
   And sympathise with those strange things that lie
In other lives ; but soon the vision ends,
   And they are curtained off again to be
   Alone, as they were born and soon must die.

THE TRAVELLER.

He laid him down beneath a spreading tree,
  And said, ' The journey is not worth the pain ;
  I cannot suffer all the toil and strain
To reach some distant goal I do not see.
Here will I wait and watch the crowds that flee
  From their distempered dreams, and never gain
  The haven they have sought so long in vain.
The sight perhaps may yield a smile for me.'

But one came by, who turned her glowing eyes
  Full on his face, and beckoned him away.
  His soul was weary ; he would far prefer
To rest in scornful ease, and still despise
Delusive hopes ;—and yet he could not stay,
  But rose and went, that he might be with her.

NORTH DEVON.

Once more doth fortune suffer me to rest
  My limbs, which falter in the paths I tread,—
  To halt awhile, and sink my weary head
In slumber on the moorland's maiden breast,
Where the sweet voices linger that have blessed
  My bygone years, and all my thoughts are led
  To memories that counted with the dead,
Save when a breeze just reached me from the West.

Fair, lonely land!—thy laughing streamlets greet
  My coming with their gayest minstrelsy ;
Thy climbing mists creep up to kiss my feet
  From wooded combes, whose whisper speaks to me
Of unforgetting, friendly hearts that beat
  Here, in the murmur of the Severn Sea.

IN NOVEMBER.

GREAT deathless Soul, that dwellest all unseen
   Beyond the changing spectacle of Time,
   Thou breathest a significance sublime
Into this corpse of beauty that has been,—
These damp, dead leaves which mark the withering
     green,
   Like crusted bloodstains of some gloomy crime,—
   These mournful shapes of pallid mist, which climb
On fir-clad crest and heather-lined ravine.

In stately tints of juniper and yew
   Thine everlasting life is figured plain ;
I know that thou wilt change the sombre hue
   Of winter ;—yet, though boughs be bright again
With clustered leaves, their glory will be new,—
   Not this old splendour that has now been slain.

THE GOLDFIELD.

WITH mouths that taste despair, and haggard eyes,
  The weary crowd bends to its thankless toil ;
  They crush the quartz and sift the sterile soil,
And, here and there, one gains the long-sought prize ;
But, oftener, the flag half-lowered flies
  Of lost, dead hopes it pleases Fate to foil ;
  So many share the fray,—so few the spoil,—
We wonder where the corpse of Justice lies.

Poor coward ! Wilt thou falter and lament
  Since Fortune's empty echoes mock thy call ?
Yonder great rock, which shades thy flimsy tent
  Has seen a million summers rise and fall
Unmoved thereby ; is the last sunbeam spent ?
  Life lasts,—hope lives,—and these are worth it all.

IN WESTMINSTER ABBEY.

LONDON's dark cloak is wrapped around her head,
   And noonday here has blurred in spurious night
   Dim arch and dusky pillar ; yellow light
From lonely gas-jets flickering is shed
Mocking the marble records of the dead,
   Like Fame, so hardly gathered in the fight,
   Faded so soon.—What lives beneath the blight ?
Some empty names by careless idlers read.

Men called you mighty once, whose fervent breath
   Could move the world to labour, laugh, or weep;
And now the last remembrance perisheth
   Of that which seemed to strike its roots so deep.
All are but shadows ;—nought endures, save Death,
   Which also is a shadow, cast by sleep.

A BALLROOM FANCY.

SPLENDOUR of costly raiment, precious stones,
  Lit by the long wax candles on the wall,
  Whose beams upon the smiling faces fall,—
Soft hair and gleaming bosoms,—flashing zones
  Of jewels,—music's most voluptuous tones,—
  Eyes that enchant and voices that enthrall,—
  Beauty, and wealth, and highest rank, and all
The imagination of the world enthrones.

Was it to set these human gems in gold
  That God made man, with all his griefs and joys?
Has the great chariot of Time been rolled,
  With weary travellers, through dust and noise
Of such long ages, that they might behold
  These grown-up children playing with their toys?

SUNSET.

THE pale, smooth surface of this northern sea
  Darkens and deepens, like a crystal thought
  Within some quiet brain serenely wrought,
On which descends the shrouding mystery
Of fancy, and the painted dreams that we
  With passion-throb and burning hearts have bought,
  And softens tint and shade and shape, till nought
Remains but purple mist and memory.

Vague in the dusk dim-featured headlands loom,
  Like swollen fingers of a spectral hand
Laid on the water shining through the gloom ;
  And, in a tongue we may not understand,
I hear the ghostly messenger of doom
  Speak through the waves that froth upon the sand.

SYMPATHY.

OH, woman-heart !—mine answered when you beat,
  Sharing your burden with a kindred load
  Of half-remembered phantoms, as we rode
On through the valley, where our horses' feet
Sent the sharp echoes wandering to greet
  The soft descending shadows ;—crimson glowed
  A flaming sunset on the clouds, and showed
Through gauze-like mist the landscape smiling sweet.

No thought of love between us !—but the spell
  Of dreaming hill-top and enchanted wood
Throbbed in each bosom like a distant bell,
  Binding our souls in one mysterious mood,
Till from our eyes the scales of darkness fell,
  And, for a little space, we understood.

TRISTRAM.

HERE in the dark alone, I dream of you,
  Whose presence could bring back to me the sun ;
  Imperious rebellion has begun
To shake the sombre happiness I knew
In finding one so steadfast and so true ;
  Patient beneath the tangle Fate had spun,
  With strength which shamed me, till I dared not
      shun
The deed of sacrifice you bade me do.

What prize shall be my recompence for this ?
  I ask no fairer gift from Heaven or Hell
To feed my soul's strong hunger than the bliss
  Whose weight you suffered me to learn so well,
The sweet, responsive passion of your kiss,
  And on my breast your bosom's stormy swell.

A SINGER'S DESTINY.

To stand amidst the shadows all too long ;—
    To watch the heedless worldlings saunter by,
    Whose hearts might echo his forsaken cry,
Could they but hear its passion beating strong
Against the fretful murmur of the throng ;—
    To wait while youth, and hope, and vigour die ;—
    To fill the hollow vastness of the sky
With unprevailing agonies of song.

It may be that he lacks the essential flame ;
    It may be that the music of his lyre
Shall earn a scroll of splendour for his name,
    Printed in deathless characters of fire ;—
But worn-out hope will steal the power from Fame
    To satisfy his impotent desire.

DUPED.

'SOME day' he said, ' I shall begin to live.'
  Year after year he said it, and the thought
  Gave comfort ;—hitherto his life had caught
No golden pleasure, like an empty sieve
Letting the sand run through it ; negative
  And dull the hours had drifted by, with nought
  Of all the glowing loveliness he sought,
Which Fate so steadfastly refused to give.

But all at once he woke and realised
  How far and fast the silent years had flown,
And how those unsubstantial things he prized
  Had glided ghostlike on, nor ever shown
Their faces in the season he despised,—
  For he was living then,—and had not known.

A NIGHT JOURNEY.

Red sunset flaring on a northern land
  Of moor and mountain ; then the dusk,—and white
  Of yon dim sea, losing its hoarded light ;
Then darkened slopes and valleys on each hand,
Where dense trees, girt with shrouds of vapour, stand,
  While pallid stars grow clearer to the sight,
  And purple sky yet deepens into night,
Till moonrise powders all with silver sand.

Great calm,—and memories of vanished years,
  With the sweet, faded burdens that they bore,—
An aftermath of youthful hopes and tears,
  As through the night the swift wheels rock and roar.
But the last hour a lurid spectre rears,—
  And then the flaming, squalid streets once more.

CHOICE.

If men had power to choose their fate, you think
    Life's music could not tempt you to be born?—
    I ask your pardon if a shade of scorn
Rings in my question;—you would rather sink
Than face the toil of swimming!—you would shrink
    From every rose that nestled on a thorn!—
    Sooner than taste the homely cup of horn,
However sweet the wine, you would not drink?

Grant me your leave to differ!—I have played
    The cards as they were dealt me. When I lost
I cursed my luck most heartily—and paid.
    But if some turn of Fortune's wheel has tossed
Red gold into my lap, I have not weighed
    The price of winning.—It is worth the cost.

LONDON: HATCHARD, PICCADILLY.

www.ingramcontent.com/pod-product-compliance
Lightning Source LLC
Chambersburg PA
CBHW030837300326
41935CB00037B/590